I0163900

MAKING
DISCIPLES

THE GREATEST MISSION OF MANKIND

HAMP LEE III

(com)mission
PUBLISHING

Copyright © 2014, 2017 by Hamp Lee III

All rights reserved. No part of this publication may be re-
produced, distributed or transmitted in any form or by any
means, including photocopying, recording, or other elec-
tronic or mechanical methods, without the prior written
permission of the publisher, except in the case of brief quo-
tations embodied in critical reviews and certain other non-
commercial uses permitted by copyright law. For permission
requests, write to the publisher at info@commissionpubs.-
com.

DISCLAIMER: The material in this book is intended for
educational purposes only While the author has made every
attempt to verify that the information provided in this book
is correct and up to date, the author assumes no responsibil-
ity for any error, inaccuracy, or outcome from the application of this material.

All scripture references used in this book are from the
KING JAMES BIBLE.

Making Disciples: The Greatest Mission of Mankind
Hamp Lee III -- 2nd ed.

IBSN 978-1-940042-58-9

CONTENTS

MATTHEW 28:18–20

And Jesus came and spake unto them, saying, All power is given unto me in heaven and in earth. Go ye therefore, and teach all nations, baptizing them in the name of the Father, and of the Son, and of the Holy Ghost: Teaching them to observe all things whatsoever I have commanded you: and, lo, I am with you always, even unto the end of the world. Amen.

INTRODUCTION

God has a mission to save His creation. Through His love and forgiveness, He desires to save all men and bring them into the knowledge of the truth. And one of the ways God reveals His love and forgiveness is through disciples.

Disciples are followers of Jesus—students, learners, and pupils of His commands. Through their obedience to Jesus' commands, they reflect God's love and character. As disciples reflect God's love and character, God is glorified and many come to know Him personally.

My purpose in writing *Making Disciples: The Greatest Mission of Mankind* is to share several principles for making disciples. I will first address what it means to be a disciple of Jesus before discussing the nature of godly relationships; how godly relationships create the perfect environment for making disciples; and outline several ways to model, teach, and encourage obedience to Jesus' commands within godly relationships.

I pray *Making Disciples: The Greatest Mission of Mankind* will not only help you become the disciple Jesus intends, but will empower you with the means to make disciples of others. May this book become a great resource and blessing in your life and ministry.

BEING A DISCIPLE

As disciples follow Jesus, they each make a personal commitment to learn, study, and obey Jesus' commands. The commitment each disciple makes cannot be haphazard or without the understanding of what it means to be His disciple.

When a person desires to be a disciple of Jesus, it is important for him or her to consider the cost associated with following Him. In Luke 14:25–33, Jesus explains what it means to be His disciple and the cost associated with that decision:

And there went great multitudes with him: and he turned, and said unto them, If any man come to me, and hate not his father, and mother, and wife, and children, and brethren, and sisters, yea, and his own life also, he cannot be my disciple. And whosoever doth not bear his cross, and come after me, cannot be my disciple. For which of you, intending to build a tower, sitteth not down first, and counteth the cost, whether he have sufficient to fin-

ish it? Lest haply, after he hath laid the foundation, and is not able to finish it, all that behold it begin to mock him, Saying, This man began to build, and was not able to finish. Or what king, going to make war against another king, sitteth not down first, and consulteth whether he be able with ten thousand to meet him that cometh against him with twenty thousand? Or else, while the other is yet a great way off, he sendeth an ambassage, and desireth conditions of peace. So likewise, whosoever he be of you that forsaketh not all that he hath, he cannot be my disciple.

Jesus says that if any man does not hate his father, mother, wife, children, brothers, sisters, and even his own life, he cannot be His disciple. The word hate is translated in Luke 14:26 as to detest; to love less.[1] Hating one's self is a total surrender (or giving up) of his or her connections to the world: lusts of the flesh to satisfy human appetites; lustful eyes that are envious or covetous; and the pride of life (boastful, arrogant behavior).

1 JOHN 2:15–17

Love not the world, neither the things that are in the world. If any man love the world, the love of the Father is not in him. For all that is in the world, the lust of the flesh, and the lust of the eyes, and the pride of life, is not of the Father, but is of the world. And the world passeth away, and the lust thereof: but he that doeth the will of God abideth for ever.

As you hate those closest to you and your own life, you must also bear your cross and follow Jesus. Bearing your cross is a figurative example for the assignment, purpose, or work God has called you to complete. Any connections to the world and/or loving others above God will interfere with your ability to complete your assignment, purpose, or work.[2] Just as Jesus carried His cross and was obedient to His purpose on earth, you too must follow Him through obedience.[3]

Becoming a disciple of Jesus is the most important decision you will make in your life. This decision should not be taken lightly. Whether or not this is the first time you have heard about being a disciple or the cost of discipleship, please take a few days to review this chapter (and specifically Luke 14:25–33) before continuing any further. In your thoughts and meditation, consider (1) the requirements for being a disciple; (2) your understanding of the cost of discipleship; and (3) if you are ready to commit yourself to being a disciple of Jesus, based on His definition and standard.

DISCIPLES AND RELATIONSHIPS

Godly relationships create the perfect environment for making disciples.

As thousands followed Jesus during His ministry on earth, He spent the better part of His time investing in the lives of twelve men. These twelve men had not only witnessed His miracles and heard His teachings, but through Jesus' honesty, openness, and trust, He created an environment to develop and shape them in the nature and character of God.[4]

The environment for making disciples is established through godly relationships. Godly relationships are founded in love and built on honesty, openness, and trust. And through these attributes (and several others listed on the following pages), disciples can experience environments where God is glorified; God's Word is routinely discussed and used in practical application; godliness is encouraged and modeled; and an emphasis for making disciples is prominent.

Attributes of Godly Relationships

Love

PROVERBS 17:17
A friend loveth at all times, and a brother is born for adversity.

MATTHEW 22:36–40
Master, which is the great commandment in the law? Jesus said unto him, Thou shalt love the Lord thy God with all thy heart, and with all thy soul, and with all thy mind. This is the first and great commandment. And the second is like unto it, Thou shalt love thy neighbour as thyself. On these two commandments hang all the law and the prophets.

LUKE 6:31
And as ye would that men should do to you, do ye also to them likewise.

JOHN 13:34–35
A new commandment I give unto you, That ye love one another; as I have loved you, that ye also love

one another. By this shall all men know that ye are
my disciples, if ye have love one to another.

1 CORINTHIANS 13:3–7
Charity suffereth long, and is kind; charity envieth
not; charity vaunteth not itself, is not puffed
up, Doth not behave itself unseemly, seeketh not her
own, is not easily provoked, thinketh no evil; Re-
joiceth not in iniquity, but rejoiceth in the
truth; Beareth all things, believeth all things, hopeth
all things, endureth all things.

1 JOHN 3:18
My little children, let us not love in word, neither
in tongue; but in deed and in truth.

Honesty, Openness, and Trust

PROVERBS 16:28
A froward man soweth strife: and a whisperer sepa-
rateth chief friends.

PROVERBS 27:6
Faithful are the wounds of a friend; but the kisses of
an enemy are deceitful.

ROMANS 12:17
Recompense to no man evil for evil. Provide things
honest in the sight of all men.

2 CORINTHIANS 4:1–7

Therefore seeing we have this ministry, as we have received mercy, we faint not; But have renounced the hidden things of dishonesty, not walking in craftiness, nor handling the word of God deceitfully; but by manifestation of the truth commending ourselves to every man's conscience in the sight of God. But if our gospel be hid, it is hid to them that are lost: In whom the god of this world hath blinded the minds of them which believe not, lest the light of the glorious gospel of Christ, who is the image of God, should shine unto them. For we preach not ourselves, but Christ Jesus the Lord; and ourselves your servants for Jesus' sake. For God, who commanded the light to shine out of darkness, hath shined in our hearts, to give the light of the knowledge of the glory of God in the face of Jesus Christ. But we have this treasure in earthen vessels, that the excellency of the power may be of God, and not of us.

EPHESIANS 4:25

Wherefore putting away lying, speak every man truth with his neighbour: for we are members one of another.

Encouragement

PROVERBS 27:17
Iron sharpeneth iron; so a man sharpeneth the countenance of his friend.

HEBREWS 3:12–13
Take heed, brethren, lest there be in any of you an evil heart of unbelief, in departing from the living God. But exhort one another daily, while it is called To day; lest any of you be hardened through the deceitfulness of sin.

HEBREWS 10:24–25
And let us consider one another to provoke unto love and to good works: Not forsaking the assembling of ourselves together, as the manner of some is; but exhorting one another: and so much the more, as ye see the day approaching.

Selflessness

PHILIPPIANS 2:4
Look not every man on his own things, but every man also on the things of others.

Graceful Communications

EPHESIANS 4:29
Let no corrupt communication proceed out of your mouth, but that which is good to the use of edifying, that it may minister grace unto the hearers.

Wise Counsel

PROVERBS 15:22
Without counsel purposes are disappointed: but in the multitude of counsellers they are established.

PROVERBS 27:9
Ointment and perfume rejoice the heart: so doth the sweetness of a man's friend by hearty counsel.

THE DISCIPLE'S MATH

Prayer, Understanding People, Patience, Instruction, and Listening to the Holy Spirit

As godly relationships provide the perfect environment for discipleship, it is important to establish the purpose and function of these relationships. Godly relationships must become more than environments for fellowship. They must become vehicles for modeling, teaching, and encouraging obedience to Jesus' commands.

On the following pages, I have provided the mnemonic PUPIL (Prayer, Understanding People, Patience, Instruction, and Listening to the Holy Spirit). This mnemonic outlines the framework for deepening godly relationships by providing avenues to focus godly relationships on discipleship. With an emphasis of discipleship in godly relationships, disciples are intentionally shaped and developed to fulfill and replicate Jesus' Great Commission.

Prayer

Prayer is your conduit for communicating with God—the means for drawing intimately closer to Him. Whether mental or oral, your prayers should be as often as each breath you take.[5] As you share your life and heart with God, prayer becomes a discovery of yourself and a window into His heart and will.[6]

In the context of godly relationships and discipleship, prayer also opens channels of intercession. Intercession is a prayer request made to God concerning another person, situation, or event. Intercession is founded in love, shaped through compassion, and stirs a deep desire to see needs met, people helped, and God glorified.[7] Oftentimes, intercession is your greatest means of help and support as you await God's direction and guidance through prayer.

EPHESIANS 6:18
Praying always with all prayer and supplication in the Spirit, and watching thereunto with all perseverance and supplication for all saints

How should you pray?

MATTHEW 6:5–13

And when thou prayest, thou shalt not be as the hypocrites are: for they love to pray standing in the synagogues and in the corners of the streets, that they may be seen of men. Verily I say unto you, They have their reward. But thou, when thou prayest, enter into thy closet, and when thou hast shut thy door, pray to thy Father which is in secret; and thy Father which seeth in secret shall reward thee openly. But when ye pray, use not vain repetitions, as the heathen do: for they think that they shall be heard for their much speaking. Be not ye therefore like unto them: for your Father knoweth what things ye have need of, before ye ask him. After this manner therefore pray ye: Our Father which art in heaven, Hallowed be thy name. Thy kingdom come, Thy will be done in earth, as it is in heaven. Give us this day our daily bread. And forgive us our debts, as we forgive our debtors. And lead us not into temptation, but deliver us from evil: For thine is the kingdom, and the power, and the glory, for ever. Amen.

Not to be seen of men.

People that pray to be seen of men are considered hypocrites. They are hypocrites because they do not live by the standard they portray. Their focus is often for others to see how 'spiritual' they seem (pride of life). Their reward is not answered prayer, only the applause of men.

Go to a private place.

In comparison to those that pray openly to be seen of men, you should pray in secret. Pray by going in your closet (a hidden place) and shutting the door. What God sees in secret, He will answer openly.

Keep prayers short and simple.

Heathens (pagans, sinners) pray with vain repetitions. They believe they will be heard because of their self-admiring repetitions and long prayers. Though Jesus encourages us to pray always, He says not to be like them because your Father already knows what you need.[8]

Pray in this manner...

Our Father which art in heaven, hallowed be thy name.

As you enter into prayer, begin by acknowledging your Father in heaven. Hallowed (holy, set apart) is His Name. God is to be honored, worshipped, and revered in your mind and heart and on your lips.

Thy kingdom come, thy will be done in earth, as it is in heaven.

In praying for the Kingdom of God to come and God's will to be done, you are praying for His Kingdom to be advanced around the world by His Spirit. As the Kingdom of God dwells within the hearts of believers, they have the ability to live in conformity to God's standard of obedience and holiness.[9]

Give us this day our daily bread.

Here, you are asking God for today's provisions and not your provisions for tomorrow or the next year. Your desire should not be to receive so much where you forget God or too little where you want to steal.[10]

And forgive us our debts, as we forgive our debtors.

Ask God to forgive you for your sins only as you forgive those that sin against you. Forgiving someone of his or her sins against you is treating him or her as if he or she never wronged you.

MATTHEW 6:14–15
For if ye forgive men their trespasses, your heavenly Father will also forgive you: But if ye forgive not men their trespasses, neither will your Father forgive your trespasses.

If you have been unwilling to forgive someone, speak to God about your reasons for holding onto unforgiveness.[11] Be honest and pour out the pain and emotions flowing through your mind and heart. As you do this, remain open to His Word and wise counsel.

The cure for unforgiveness is meditating on God's Word. Without meditating on His Word, pride, anger, bitterness, and hate will flood your mind and heart and direct your actions.[12] However, meditating on God's Word will ignite your faith, renew your mind, and usher a response of forgiveness through obedience.[13]

JAMES 1:19–25
Wherefore, my beloved brethren, let every man be swift to hear, slow to speak, slow to wrath: For the wrath of man worketh not the righteousness of God. Wherefore lay apart all filthiness and superfluity of naughtiness, and receive with meekness the engrafted word, which is able to save your souls. But be ye doers of the word, and not hearers only, deceiving

your own selves. For if any be a hearer of the word, and not a doer, he is like unto a man beholding his natural face in a glass: For he beholdeth himself, and goeth his way, and straightway forgetteth what manner of man he was. But whoso looketh into the perfect law of liberty, and continueth therein, he being not a forgetful hearer, but a doer of the work, this man shall be blessed in his deed.

Lead us not into temptation.

When times of temptation come, God will show you a way of escape.[14] Sometimes the way of escape will require you to remove yourself from a physical location or mentally or emotionally disengage from a specific person or issue. God is willing to deliver you, but you must be willing to take the path He reveals to you.[15]

Closing.

At the conclusion of your prayer, acknowledge the Kingdom (rule), power (ability), and glory (honor, exaltation, and preeminence) of your Father in heaven—forever.

Understanding People

Understanding people can be one of the most challenging endeavors you may face. As humans have a complex range of emotions, thoughts, and ideals, many people find it easier to treat others the way they want. They do not take the time or make the investment to understand anyone. They only want people to understand them and their way of doing things.

However, in building godly relationships and making disciples, it is important that you take the time to understand people. When you understand people, you are empowered with the knowledge to cultivate deeper relationships. And the deeper your relationship, the greater your ability to influence and impact their lives in discipleship. Now, in order to cultivate deeper relationships, there are several things you should first consider:

Sinners Sin.

Jesus was known as a friend of sinners.[16] In His interactions, He brought healing, support, and redemption through forgiveness for many people without judgment. For example, when a woman was caught in the act of adultery, she was brought to Jesus by the scribes and Pharisees in order to tempt Him.[17] Though their law required her to be stoned, Jesus began writing on the ground as if He did not hear them. Jesus then stood up and said, "*He that is without sin among you, let him first cast a stone at her,*" then stooped down again to write. Convicted by their own conscience, one by one, they departed until only Jesus and the woman remained. Jesus stood up again and asked where her accusers were and if there was any man to condemn her. As she answered "*No man, Lord,*" Jesus would not condemn her either. He told her, "*Neither do I condemn thee: go, and sin no more.*"

Even though the woman was deserving of punishment, Jesus showed mercy, compassion, and forgiveness. Like Jesus, you can show mercy and compassion toward others when they are in the midst of sinful acts or behavior. Just as someone may have looked past your sinful behavior to show you a better future with Jesus, you can do the same for others. However, in your interactions with them, do not place yourself in tempting or sinful situations where you compromise your testimony or standing with God.[18]

Have a listening ear.

JAMES 1:19–20
Wherefore, my beloved brethren, let every man be swift to hear, slow to speak, slow to wrath: For the wrath of man worketh not the righteousness of God.

Everyone has a story. And every story is important. Many people are willing to share their life stories, but have few outlets to do so. Sadly, many in our society do not have the time, patience, or interest to learn the story of another person. However, by taking the time to hear someone's life story, you learn more about him or her and discover ways to deepen your relationship.

Understanding positions and perspectives.

As everyone has a story, everyone has an opinion, perspective, or position. And as such, it is important to allow people to freely express their views— even if they are in opposition to yours. People should be free to share their thoughts without fear of reprisal, coercion, or disassociation. When you allow people the opportunity to express themselves freely, you establish environments of honesty, openness, and trust—the inroads toward godly relationships and discipleship. These inroads often reveal the most appropriate avenues for helping disciples grow and develop.

Do not judge.

MATTHEW 7:1–2
Judge not, that ye be not judged. For with what judgment ye judge, ye shall be judged: and with what measure ye mete, it shall be measured to you again.

The word judge is translated in Matthew 7:1 as to distinguish, i.e., decide (mentally or judicially); by implication, to try, condemn, punish: avenge, conclude, condemn, decree, determine, call in question.[19] If you become judgmental, you lose the ability to show love or compassion. You simply pronounce your 'sentence' and move on. However, compassion activates a desire to genuinely help others and reflect the love of God.

Patience

EPHESIANS 4:2–3
With all lowliness and meekness, with longsuffering, forbearing one another in love; Endeavouring to keep the unity of the Spirit in the bond of peace.

The earth was not built in a day and neither will disciples. Like planting a seed in the ground and waiting for it to grow, you will need to exercise patience in your godly relationships.[20] Patience allows you to walk with others as they learn how to work out their salvation and live as disciples.[21]

GALATIANS 6:9
And let us not be weary in well doing: for in due season we shall reap, if we faint not.

Pray, plant seeds of love, and be a source of encouragement, help, and support when needed. But remember not to place yourself in tempting or compromising situations in your desire to help others. Be guided by the Holy Spirit.

Instruction

2 TIMOTHY 3:16–17
All scripture is given by inspiration of God, and is profitable for doctrine, for reproof, for correction, for instruction in righteousness: That the man of God may be perfect, thoroughly furnished unto all good works.

Instruction encompasses elements of learning sound doctrine, living according to sound doctrine, and teaching sound doctrine. Each element is necessary to help disciples in their growth and development.[22]

Learning Sound Doctrine.

2 TIMOTHY 2:15
Study to shew thyself approved unto God, a workman that needeth not to be ashamed, rightly dividing the word of truth.

All disciples must be committed to reading, studying, and meditating on God's Word. Reading assists disciples in understanding the meaning, truth, and power of God's Word. Studying God's Word is more in-depth than reading, as it offers opportunities to delve into the intricacies of scripture for greater clarity and understanding. Meditation is a slow and intentional view of scripture that allow disciples to continually set their minds (thinking) on what they read and study.[23]

For learning sound doctrine, I have written three books for instructing disciples. The first book, *Advancing the Kingdom: God's Plan for Redeeming His Creation*, reviews the entire biblical message from the perspective of the Kingdom of God. From the creation of the earth and man, the birth and purpose of Jesus, to the means of entering eternal life with God, *Advancing the Kingdom:*

God's Plan for Redeeming His Creation provides a simple, yet complete overview for understanding God's will for mankind.

The second book, *Living for the Kingdom: Teaching What Jesus Taught*, is a devotional study outlining the life, teachings, and commands of Jesus. Structured as a devotional study guide covering one hundred fifteen lessons, *Living for the Kingdom: Teaching What Jesus Taught*, outlines the cost of discipleship, the characteristics of disciples, and the commands disciples are to follow.

The third book, *The Bible Study Blueprint: An Essential Guide for Studying God's Word* provides specific methods for studying passages of scripture. You will learn how to find a scripture's historical and personal context, conduct in-depth word searches, develop detailed outlines, and build personal profiles.

Each book can be used for personal or group studies. They are available on my website as free PDFs and through other online outlets such as Amazon, iBooks, Google Books, and Barnes & Noble.[24]

Living According to Sound Doctrine.

ROMANS 12:1–2
I beseech you therefore, brethren, by the mercies of God, that ye present your bodies a living sacrifice, holy, acceptable unto God, which is your reasonable service. And be not conformed to this world: but be ye transformed by the renewing of your mind, that ye may prove what is that good, and acceptable, and perfect, will of God.

Living according to sound doctrine is the practical application of your reading, study, and meditation. As the mind is renewed, it is prepared for action.[25] With each circumstance, situation, and decision you encounter; you will have an opportunity to grow in godliness through practical application.[26]

1 TIMOTHY 4:12
Let no man despise thy youth; but be thou an example of the believers, in word, in conversation, in charity, in spirit, in faith, in purity.

Living according to sound doctrine is important in godly relationships because disciples need to see examples of godliness. They need to see how other disciples work out their salvation, maintain a standard of holiness unto God, and establish a good report in the world.

1 TIMOTHY 4:16
Take heed unto thyself, and unto the doctrine; continue in them: for in doing this thou shalt both save thyself, and them that hear thee.

Teaching Sound Doctrine.

Teaching sound doctrine combines the elements of learning sound doctrine and living according to sound doctrine. All three are needed in order to help disciples live in godliness.

Teaching sound doctrine involves demonstration and instruction. Demonstration presents sound doctrine in word and deed. Instruction is an extension of what is studied, learned, and shared in personal or group settings.

All disciples (including those being led in evangelistic settings) must be taught the principles of discipleship: the cost of discipleship, the characteristics of disciples, and the responsibilities disciples are to fulfill. Teaching sound doctrine should be simple, yet thorough enough to ensure quality instruction is provided and all hearers understand what is taught.

MATTHEW 13:18–23

Hear ye therefore the parable of the sower. When any one heareth the word of the kingdom, and understandeth it not, then cometh the wicked one, and catcheth away that which was sown in his heart. This is he which received seed by the way side. But he that received the seed into stony places, the same is he that heareth the word, and anon with joy receiveth it; Yet hath he not root in himself, but dureth for a while: for when tribulation or persecution ariseth because of the word, by and by he is offended. He also that received seed among the thorns is he that heareth the word; and the care of this world, and the deceitfulness of riches, choke the word, and he becometh unfruitful. But he that received seed into the good ground is he that heareth the word, and understandeth it; which also beareth fruit, and bringeth forth, some an hundredfold, some sixty, some thirty.

Listening to the Holy Spirit

JOHN 16:13–14

Howbeit when he, the Spirit of truth, is come, he will guide you into all truth: for he shall not speak of himself; but whatsoever he shall hear, that shall he speak: and he will shew you things to come. He shall glorify me: for he shall receive of mine, and shall shew it unto you.

As the Holy Spirit dwells within believers, He teaches and guides them into all truth.[27] He will only speak what He receives from the Father. He will never lie, contradict God, or go against God's Word or His nature of love.[28] He will always lead believers closer to God and His will for their lives.

If you become unsure about God's direction, take a moment to pause. Remain prayerful and patient as you wait for an answer from Him. If necessary, ask God to confirm His message and be sensitive and open to the Holy Spirit's leading.[29] However, if you become anxious, worried, or upset, you can be tempted to make a bad decision that makes your situation worse.[30]

PHILIPPIANS 4:6–7
Be anxious for nothing, but in everything by prayer and supplication with thanksgiving let your requests be made known to God. And the peace of God, which surpasses all comprehension, will guard your hearts and your minds in Christ Jesus.

CONCLUSION

Being a disciple of Jesus and making disciples is the mission of every believer. Through discipleship, God's love and character is displayed in the world, inviting more people into discipleship and the Kingdom of God. As the Kingdom of God expands, the opportunity for more people to be saved and come into the knowledge of the truth is increased.[31] And you have an important role in this mission.

In writing *Making Disciples: The Greatest Mission of Mankind*, I wanted to provide you with an overview for being a disciple while outlining fundamental principles for making disciples. I pray you will meditate on the contents of this book and allow it to become a part of your daily life as a disciple of Jesus.

As you continue your journey in discipleship, you will meet many people that need to see and experience God's love. As you connect with them via godly relationships, I pray God will give you everything you need to be a great success for His glory in the world.

God bless.

ENDNOTES

1—"Greek Lexicon :: G3404 (KJV)." Blue Letter Bible. Sowing Circle. Web. 7 Nov, 2014. http://www.blueletterbible.org/lang/lexicon/lexicon.cfm?Strongs=G3404&t=KJV.

2—Matthew 8:18–22; 1 Corinthians 7:33; 2 Timothy 2:2–4.

3—Philippians 2:1–11.

4—Matthew 20:20–28; Mark 8:31–33; Luke 9:46–50. This is not an exhaustive scriptural search.

5—Luke 18:1–7; 1 Thessalonians 5:17.

6—Psalm 139:1–18; Proverbs 5:21; Hebrews 4:13.

7—Matthew 9:36–38.

8—Matthew 6:25–34; Luke 18:1–7.

9—Luke 17:20–21.

10—Proverbs 30:7–9; Matthew 6:25–34.

11—Isaiah 1:18.

12—Mark 7:14–23.

13—Psalm 119; Romans 10:17, Romans 12:1–2; James 1:19–25.

14—1 Corinthians 10:13.

15—John 17:15; 2 Thessalonians 3:1–3; 2 Timothy 4:17–18.

16—Luke 7:34.

17—John 8:1–11.

18—Galatians 6:1–2.

19—"Greek Lexicon :: G2919 (KJV)." Blue Letter Bible. Sowing Circle. Web. 1 Nov, 2014. http://www.blueletterbible.org/lang/lexicon/lexicon.cfm?Strongs=G2919&t=KJV.

20—1 Corinthians 3:3–11.

21—Philippians 2:12.

22—Matthew 5:14–16, Matthew 28:18–20; Titus 2.

23—Joshua 1:8; Romans 12:1–2; Ephesians 4:22–25; Colossians 3:1–2; 1 Peter 1:13–15.

24—Commission Publishing http://www.commissionpubs.com

25—1 Peter 1:13–15.

26—Psalm 25:9, Psalm 119:9–16, Psalm 119:33–40; Proverbs 3:5–6, Proverbs 4:26, Proverbs 14:15, Proverbs 27:12.

27—John 14:26.

28—Numbers 23:19; 1 Corinthians 13:1–7; 1 John 4:6–10.

29—Judges 6:11–40.

30—Proverbs 19:2; Ephesians 4:26–27, Ephesians 6:11–18; James 1:19–25, James 4:7–10; 1 Peter 5:6–11.

31—1 Timothy 2:1–4.

(com)mission
PUBLISHING

www.commissionpubs.com
info@commissionpubs.com

www.ingramcontent.com/pod-product-compliance
Lightning Source LLC
Chambersburg PA
CBHW060633030426
42337CB00018B/3340